In tennis, you hit a
across a net with a

tennis court

A tennis match can be a singles match...

...or a doubles match.

Doubles can be mixed.

grass
/gras/ or /grɑːs/

A tennis court can be a grass court...

hard court

...or a hard court.

You aim to hit the tennis ball across the net without it being hit back.

But the ball must land within the court to score or it is out.

out

in

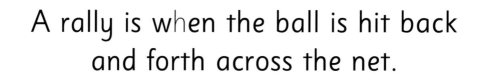

A rally is when the ball is hit back and forth across the net.

A rally can be short, just several shots, or much longer.

The longest recorded rally was 643 (six hundred and forty-three) shots!

To start, the server tosses the ball up and hits it across the court.

Serves can be very quick – more than 200mph!

The ball must not hit the net, and it must land in the serve box.

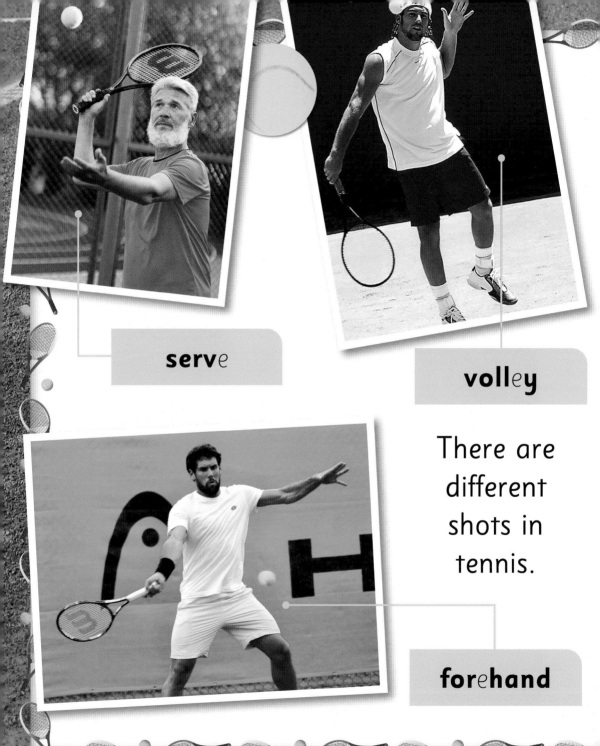

serve

volley

There are different shots in tennis.

fore**hand**

smash

lob

backhand

Wimbledon is the longest running tennis contest.

It started in 1877!